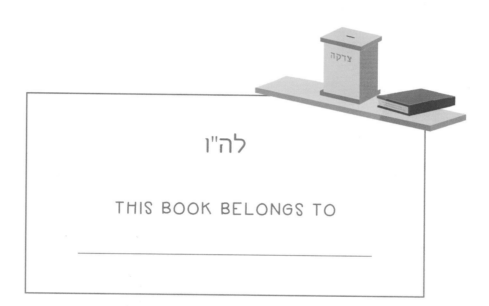

לה"ו

THIS BOOK BELONGS TO

_____

Good morning Shea!

Here is Shea, a nice Jewish boy,
starting his day with choices.

Shea's mother says,

"Don't spill your cereal and make a mess!"

His father says, "Don't forget
to say your Brochos!"

Shea looks sad and thinks, "All I
hear are so many don'ts -

DON'T! DON'T! DON'T!"

2

The bus driver says,

"Don't stand while the bus is moving."

His father says, "Don't make
any trouble in class."

Shea looks sad and thinks, "All I
hear are so many don'ts -

DON'T! DON'T! DON'T!"

Shea walks to school and all he sees are don'ts.

"Don't walk! - Don't walk!" flashes the street light.

"Don't walk on the grass"

"Don't feed the birds"

Shea looks sad and thinks, "All I see are so many don'ts -

DON'T! DN'T! DON'T!"

DON'T
WALK ON
THE GRASS!

DON'T
FEED THE
BIRDS!

4

At school, his teacher says,

"Shea - don't come late to class!"

"Don't complain about your new seat, you are late."

"Don't forget your homework!"

Shea looks sad and thinks -

"DON'T! DON'T! DON'T!"

At the playground all
he hears are don'ts.

Shea is very sad and thinks, "why
are there so many dont's?"

He wonders...

will his day get better?

Shea's Rebbi asks,

"Do you know the blessing for ice-cream?"

"Do you want to feed my pet parrot?"

"Do you want to play catch?"

Shea looks happy and says,

"Yes I do!"

His Rebbi says,

"You did a good job feeding my pet parrot!"

"You played a good game of catch!"

"You knew the blessing on ice-cream!"

Shea looks happy and says,

"So many things I can do!"

8

On his way home, Shea sees so many things he can do.

"Do walk," flashes the street light.

"Do feed the birds!"

"Do join us for a game on Sunday!"

Shea looks happy and says,

"So many things I can do!"

Shea comes home from school.

"Do you want a snack?" Mother asks.

"Do you know that I love you?"

Shea looks happy and says,

"So many things I can do!"

Shea thinks about his day.

His morning started with choices of dont's and do's, making him sad.

Shea made the right choices, making it a happy day.

I can see his smile that lasts forever.

A NOTE ABOUT THIS BOOK:

Educators, teachers, parents
and children need to listen and
recognize the challenges and choices
facing today's children. I believe
Shea's day will help in this goal.

-EH

DEDICATED TO

SHEA

and Jewish children
all over the world

Published by
KOL AVROHOM

1601 S. Fairfax Ave
Los Angeles, CA 90019
KolAvrohomKids@gmail.com